Heirs TOGETHER

SOLVING
THE MYSTERY
OF A
SATISFYING
MARRIAGE

MAC HAMMOND

KENNETH COPELAND PUBLICATIONS
FORT WORTH, TEXAS

Heirs Together

ISBN 0-88114-906-3   30-0801

©1993 Kenneth Copeland Publications

All scripture is from the *King James Version* unless otherwise noted.

Kenneth Copeland Ministries
Fort Worth, Texas 76192

Dedication

To my wife, Lynne,
with whom I am an heir together.

Contents

CHAPTER 1

Heirs Together

You can't afford to have a bad marriage. I'm firmly convinced of that.

A bad marriage will rob you of much more than happiness. It will steal your health, your wealth, and your witness. What's more, it will destroy your usefulness in the very kingdom of God itself.

That's quite a strong statement, you're thinking. *Can you back it up?*

Absolutely. Take a look with me right now at 1 Peter, chapter 3. Verse 7 says, "Likewise, ye husbands, dwell with them (your wives) according to knowledge, giving honor unto the wife, as unto a weaker vessel, being heirs together of the grace of life."

To understand that scripture, we first have to ask ourselves, what does it mean to dwell with someone "according to knowledge?" To me that simply means *according to the Word.* We, as husbands, gain knowledge about how to deal successfully with our wives through the Word of God.

Second, we must understand what is implied by the term "weaker vessel." It is simply a phrase describing the woman's physical strength. God has not equipped her physically to be the Great White Hunter or protector. Nothing more is meant.

With that said, I want you to pay special attention to the next phrase, *"...being heirs together of the grace of life."* According to the Word of God, husbands and wives inherit grace from God in this life *together*—not as individuals.

Do you want God's grace operating in your life? Well, if you're married, you'll inherit it together with your spouse or not at all! Let me repeat that. God intends for you to walk in grace, God's unmerited favor, *together* because you will not be able to walk in it any other way.

Doesn't that make you want to get serious about putting your marriage in order? I promise you, God is serious about it. If you'll read Ephesians 5:22-33, you can see why. *The marriage relationship is meant to exemplify and mirror the communion between Jesus and the Church!* That fact, in itself, is extremely significant. But verse 31 of that passage reveals something even more startling. It says, "For this cause shall a man leave his father and mother, and shall be joined unto his wife, and the two shall be one flesh." Then, immediately in verse 32 Paul says, "This is a great mystery: but I speak concerning Christ and the church."

What is the Word saying here? "For this cause...." What cause? The cause stated in verse 27—that Jesus might present to Himself a glorious Church without spot, wrinkle or blemish!

God is using marriage as an instrument to prepare a glorious Bride for Himself. That means you, as a married member of the Church universal, should also be in the process of being purified and glorified within the mysterious realm of marriage.

In other words, if your marriage isn't working, you're not going to grow from one degree of glory to another in Christ.

Husbands and wives, until you learn how to submit to one another, you'll never be able to truly submit to Christ. Until you learn to love each other as Christ loves the Church, you'll never have a right love-relationship with Jesus. Until you learn how to give yourself to each other like Jesus gives Himself to the Church, you'll not be able to partake of His giving of Himself to you.

"Alright, I'm convinced!" you say. "How do I go about making my marriage work?"

The place to start is by examining your thinking to see if you need to make any of the following three "Attitude Adjustments." No matter what kind of marriage you have right now—solid as a rock, hanging on by a thread or something in between—it can be better. You can go higher to another degree of glory. So get ready to start making the following adjustments.

Forget About Divorce

The first attitude adjustment is simple. Decide once and forever that divorce is not an option. If you continue to consider divorce as even a remote possibility, you might as well stop reading this book and go watch television, because it isn't going to do you any good.

There is simply no scriptural basis for two believers to be divorced. None. For you, divorce does not exist. You must begin to think this way.

"But what if I've already been divorced?" you ask. "Have I blown it forever?"

No. Divorce is a sin no different than any other. If you've put it under the blood of Jesus, it is gone. It will not hold you back with the Lord.

Having said that, remember this. There is no scriptural provision for two believers to get a divorce. Don't say to yourself, "I know divorce is sin, but this situation is so terrible, I'll get a divorce now and ask God to forgive me later." The Bible has very stern warnings against using God's precious grace to sin.

"But, what if I married the wrong person?" many people ask. You'd be amazed how many people the devil torments with that question.

I remember a young lady came into my office one day and insisted she had gotten out of God's will, married the wrong person, and now she was doomed to suffer until she got rid of him and found the right one. Or so she thought.

If you're thinking that way, I have good news for you. God causes all things to work together for good to those who love Christ and are called according to His purpose (Romans 8:28). Maybe you did miss God's best when you chose your spouse. Maybe you were in rebellion at the time. Perhaps you were pregnant and felt you *had* to get married.

Regardless of the circumstances, God still wants to make that marriage a glorious, fulfilling reflection of Jesus' relationship with the Church. He's committed to working that situation out for your good.

All you need to do is be determined to make it work.

Don't Try to Change Anyone but Yourself

The second attitude adjustment you may need to make is this: You must be concerned with changing no one but yourself.

Right now, take the tip of your index finger, point it at your nose, and say the following words. "I am concerned about changing no one but me."

You have just mastered the second attitude adjustment. It strikes at the heart of a major source of marriage difficulty—finger-pointing. "He always does this!" "She always does that!" Invariably, when I counsel people whose marriages are in trouble each partner tells me it's the other's fault.

No matter how exasperating your spouse may be, you can't change him. There's only one person in the world you can change and you just finished pointing at that person. It's you.

Get that through your head. You can't change your partner. As long as you keep trying, you're going to generate strife, hard feelings and pain.

Leave the Good Things Behind

Finally, there is a third attitude adjustment you must learn to make. You must forget the past.

Failure in this area is probably responsible for more marriage problems than any other single factor I've come across. One reason clinging to the past is so damaging can be found in Philippians 3:13, "Brethren, I count not myself to have apprehended: but this one thing I do, forgetting those things which are behind, and reaching forth unto those things which are before, I press toward the mark for the prize of the high calling of God in Christ Jesus."

Paul states here that forgetting the past is a prerequisite for reaching the great things in the future. This scripture applies to every area of a believer's life, including marriage. A marriage that is working the way God intends is the greatest prize you'll ever gain in this natural life.

If you keep focusing on the things behind, you'll be weighed down with the past and be prevented from pressing into the future promise of God. What do you need to forget? Only two kinds of things: the good things and the bad things.

It shocks most people when I say that. They're startled to hear they should forget the good things in their past. But strange as it sounds, it's true.

Here's why. If you dwell on how good things were in the past, you're creating in yourself dissatisfaction and resentment about the way things are now. You also open yourself up to a spirit of grief and despair. It happens all the time. Women talk about how affectionate and considerate their husbands *used* to be. How attentive he was. But now, he's just an inconsiderate louse.

Dwelling on the good things in the past will distort your perception of the present and undermine your hope for the future. Don't do it.

The only parts of your past the Bible tells you to remember are the victories you've experienced in Christ Jesus. Nothing else. Meditating on how God has delivered us from trouble in the past increases our confidence and faith for future challenges. So, next time you want to reminisce, think about that.

Leave the Bad Behind, Too

For some people, forgetting the good is no problem. It's forgetting the bad things that is really tough. But, tough or not, it must be done. If it's not, those bad memories will invariably produce the fruit of unforgiveness—toward yourself, your spouse or toward God.

In order to forgive, you must forget. According to Isaiah 43:25, even God must forget in order to forgive. "I, even I, am he that blotteth out thy transgressions for mine own sake, and will not remember thy sins."

How can you forget those painful memories and leave them behind once and for all? You must do two things.

The key to the first is in Philippians, chapter 4. "Finally, brethren, whatsoever things are true, whatsoever things are honest, whatsoever things are just, whatsoever things are pure, whatsoever things are lovely, whatsoever things are of good report; if there be any virtue and if there be any praise, think on these things" (verse 8).

You can be sure the devil will remind you of every rotten, insensitive thing your spouse has ever done. When he does, you must redirect your thinking to something good. Start looking with your eye of faith at what he or she is going to be like when they're more like Jesus.

The second thing you must do to forget the bad in your past is to stop basing your actions on it. The book of James says if you want the Word of God to work for you, you have to do more than hear it, you have to act on it. That works in the negative too. If you want to stop dwelling on the past, you must start acting like it never happened!

For example, I heard a lady give her testimony a few years ago about how God restored her marriage. Early in their marriage her husband had been unfaithful and she had found out about it. Later, after he had gotten saved, he repented of it, but she couldn't seem to forget about it.

Although they never talked about the affair, her unforgiveness manifested itself in the marriage bed. She just couldn't seem to give herself to him freely and completely. Her constant memories of his infidelity caused her to be cold toward him and it was affecting their entire relationship.

One day, God dealt with her in a prayer meeting. She decided she was going to quit acting on the basis of that 15-year-old hurt.

She went home, dolled herself up, and started giving herself to her husband without reservation. It broke the power of that incident in her past. She was free...free to forget and forgive.

There they are—three attitude adjustments that will put you in a position to receive all the things you need to make your marriage prosper. Start putting them into practice today. But don't stop there. Read on. In the following pages you find a wealth of principles and practical truths that will put you on the road to discovering firsthand what it really means to be "heirs together of the grace of life!"

CHAPTER 2

Understanding the Divine Differences

Warning: What you're about to read in this chapter may startle you.

With the help of God's Word, I'm about to explode some of the traditions and religious myths you may have picked up about marriage over the years. But if you'll keep an open mind, you'll come away with some truths about marriage that will bring you into more blessing and happiness than you ever dreamed possible.

In the Beginning

To find those truths, we need to go all the way back to the beginning, to the very first marriage on earth. We find it, of course, in Genesis 1:26-27: "And God said, Let us *make* man in our image, after our likeness: and let them have dominion over...all the earth... So God *created* man in his own image, in the image of God created he him; male and female created he them."

Most of us have read that passage many times and we think we understand it. But a quick word study reveals that much of the truth in it has been lost.

For instance, the word translated "make" in verse 26 ("let us make man in our image") is the Hebrew word *asah. Asah* literally means "to make something from material that already exists" or "to mold with the hands." The Bible uses that word there because verse 26 is referring to the construction of Adam's *body.* God made that body with the dust of the earth (something that already existed).

But the scripture uses a completely different word in the next verse where it says God "created" man in his own image. The Hebrew word translated "created" is *bara*. It means to make something from a substance that has never existed before.

Now ask yourself—what parts of man were made out of something that never existed before? His spirit and soul. Verse 27 is referring to the creation of man's soul and spirit! With that in mind, let's look at it again: "So God created man in his own image, in the image of God created he him; male and female created he them."

Notice that last phrase, "male and female created he them" occurs only there in verse 27, where the scripture refers to the creation of the soul and spirit. Verse 26 which refers to the creation of bodies doesn't say anything about the male and female.

What am I saying? Just this: When God first created man, He created *one body—not two.* That one body housed all the emotional, spiritual and intellectual characteristics of both male and female.

We see confirmation of this idea in Genesis 5, verses 1 and 2: "In the day that God created man, in the likeness of God made he him; *male and female* created he them; and blessed them, and called their name Adam, in the day when they were created."

This verse clearly states that when God made the first man, he made him "male and female" and called their name Adam. God made the first man complete! Every attribute and component of humanity was placed in Adam. It was that complete man, possessing the attributes of both male and female, that was "in the image and likeness of God." It was that complete man that God gave "dominion" over the earth (Genesis 1:27-28).

I know this may seem quite bizarre to many of you reading this right now. But if you are going to understand God's divine plan for marriage, you're going to have to get rid of those religious traditions and ideas you've carried since childhood. We were told cute little creation stories that weren't grounded in the reality of God's Word.

"And the Two Shall Become One Flesh..."

At this point, you may be asking yourself, "If all this is true and God had such a perfect creation all in one package at the start, why did He separate woman from man?"

That's a good question. You'll find the answer in Genesis 2:18: "The Lord God said, It is not good that the man should be alone...."

Most people think this verse says that God suddenly woke up, discovered Adam was all by himself and decided to make him a companion. That sounds very sweet but it is just plain wrong.

Adam wasn't all by himself! He had the fellowship of God. So what the Bible is telling us here is Adam had fallen out of that fellowship. Yes, even before he sinned, Adam had lost his intimacy with his Heavenly Father! He *must* have—otherwise he would not have been alone.

How can I be so sure? Look at John 8 and you'll see. There, Jesus says, "...I am not alone, but I and the Father that sent me...the Father hath not left me alone; for I do always those things that please him" (verses 16, 29).

The reason Jesus was not alone was that he has a relationship with the Father. God was His companion. Adam was originally designed to share that same kind of divine companionship, but something went wrong.

Even before the Fall had taken place...even before Adam had eaten of the fruit of the tree of knowledge of good and evil...he stopped doing the things that pleased the Father. Thus, he was alone.

Rather than leave man in that isolated state, Genesis 2:21-22, tells us: "...the Lord God caused a deep sleep to fall upon Adam and he slept; and he took one of his ribs, closed up the flesh instead thereof; And the rib, which the Lord God had taken from the man, *made* he a woman, and brought her unto the man."

The word "made" that is used here to describe the creation of Eve isn't like either of the other two Hebrew words we've seen. The word here is *banah*. It means skillfully or artistically formed. That says something wonderful about you ladies, doesn't it? Woman is twice removed from the dust of the earth—doubly refined.

But note that the word *bara,* for creation of soul and spirit, isn't used for Eve. Why? Because God had already created the female personality. It was housed in the body called Adam! God simply extracted that personality and put it in the new body He had formed from Adam's rib.

God's separation of Woman out of Man created an unprecedented situation. For the first time in creation, a being was incomplete. Although both man and woman were separate and distinct entities, neither one was completely "in the image and likeness of God" any longer. Neither one of them alone was able to walk in the dominion over the earth God had originally granted them.

But God's intention was not for them to remain in that state of incompletion. That's why He decreed: "Therefore shall a man leave his father and his mother, and shall cleave unto his wife: and they shall be one flesh" (Genesis 2:24).

God created Holy Matrimony. He joined man and a woman together by the miracle-working power of the Holy Spirit, transforming them once more into the image and likeness of God and creating the completion that entitled them to dominion over the earth.

Once you understand that, you'll see why marriage is so vital to God's plan for mankind. You'll also understand why Satan is so determined to destroy it.

When a man and a woman marry, a new creature comes into existence—a being that never existed before. That's what the Bible means by "one flesh." It is referring to the restoration of the completeness of Adam's original state—a state in which all of the elements that constitute "male" and "female" were housed in one body.

Which Way to the Tree of Life?

We've already seen that one reason God separated Woman from Man was because it was not good for Man to be alone. But there was also another reason.

In Genesis 2:16-17 we read: "And the Lord God commanded the man, saying, Of every tree of the garden thou mayest freely eat: But of the tree of the knowledge of good and evil, thou shalt not eat...."

Notice God encouraged Adam to eat of *all* the other trees of the garden. One of those trees was the Tree of Life.

The Tree of Life throughout the Word of God is a type or symbol of Jesus Christ. It's a type of the divine nature. We are told in the New Covenant to become partakers of the divine nature. And eating of the Tree of Life was the way Adam was to have partaken in the divine nature. But he didn't do it. How do we know?

We know because after the Fall, God said, "Behold, the man is become as one of us, to know good and evil; and now, *lest he put forth his hand, and take also of the tree of life, and eat,* and live forever..." (Genesis 3:22).

Obviously, Adam had not yet partaken of the Tree of Life. His failure to do so shows us one of the most basic reasons God created woman. He created her to point her man toward the Tree of Life.

Adam alone didn't take enough interest in the Tree of Life (spiritual things) to make the walk to the center of the garden where the tree was. The same is true today. In their natural state, left to their own devices, men are not likely to pursue the things of God. Generally they need the outside influence or encouragement of women.

Now, I'm not saying men are spiritual lunkheads who can never hear the voice of God (although some of you wives may think so). I'm simply saying that God created the male to be concerned with certain types of practical things essential to the success of God's new creation.

God gave the male a drive to produce and reproduce, to provide for and protect his family. He placed these drives deep inside him so this new creation called Mankind would thrive and prosper. The pitfall is that in pursuit of those things, a man can lose his sensitivity to spiritual things. His wife, however, is designed to help him avoid that pitfall.

A man who doesn't understand this principle often ends up resenting his wife's preoccupation with the things of God. "Who does she think she is, anyway?" he'll grumble. "Miss Super-spiritual?"

He may even try to compete with her. Many times, for example, the wife gets saved first and starts moving on with God so quickly that the husband is left behind to "eat her dust" (spiritually speaking, of course). Then he hears he's supposed to be the head of the household. Since he's already irritated about her jumping out ahead, the next time she comes to tell him she's heard from God, he just shuts her down.

"I'm the head of this house!" he'll say. "If God needs to tell us something, He can tell *me!*" (The odds are, God *did* try to tell him but he wasn't listening as intently as his wife was.)

Men, get smart! When you start to slip into that kind of resentment, stop and remember why God created your wife. He created her because you need help getting to the Tree of Life. So start listening to her!

Now ladies, that doesn't give you license to nag your husband about spiritual things. That's the surest way I know to send him in the other direction. Don't nag. Pray for your man. Believe God where he's concerned. Encourage him. Exhort him.

First Peter 3:1 says you can win your husband without saying a word. In other words, you can point him toward the Tree of Life without nagging. I know, because my wife did it for me.

When we first went into the ministry, I felt like a duck out of water. I had no Bible college, no theology degree, nothing! I felt tremendously insecure. But my wife encouraged and exhorted me. She never magnified my obvious shortcomings. She never told me how unspiritual I was. She prayed for me and believed God would continue the work He had begun in me.

Whatever fruit my ministry has borne to this point is attributable to her. I know there's still a lot of room for improvement in me, but she's working on it. And she'll get me there!

Deception Protection

Before all you wives go charging full speed ahead pulling your husband along behind you, let me warn you of something. You have a weakness. Because of your spiritual sensitivity, ladies, you're also much more likely to be deceived. Yes, the very same receptiveness that makes you so open to the things of God, makes you an easier target for the devil's lies. That was demonstrated at the Fall.

Paul tells us Eve was deceived by the serpent but Adam was not. Adam knew exactly what he was doing. He simply chose to follow his woman rather than obey God. Don't get the wrong idea. Women aren't easily deceived about just anything. It's in spiritual things that they are vulnerable.

You can see evidence of that vulnerability in many churches today. Most of the time when a group of intercessors, for example, get off into some kind of weird teachings and activities, you'll generally find women at the center of it. I don't say that to demean women in any way. I just say it to encourage them to beware and keep in balance.

With that in mind, ladies, when you feel God has spoken to you about something, go to your husband. Ask him to pray about it with you. He may come to you a few days later and say, "Honey, I've taken this matter to the Lord and I believe you're wrong. I believe to do that thing would be a trap, so we're going to do something else instead."

When that happens, support him in the decision he has made. Remember that God has given him to you as an anchor to keep you from getting drawn off course.

The sum of what I'm saying is this: Husbands, you need to understand that without your wife, you're incomplete. Without her, your chances of getting to the Tree of Life are greatly diminished. You need to involve her in the decisions you make and you must respect and acknowledge her spiritual sensitivity.

Wives, you must realize that your husband is the one who keeps you from falling into deception and who complements you in every way. So when he makes a decision—even if you disagree—you need to respect it.

Having that kind of mutual appreciation operating in a marriage—each partner knowing that he or she is incomplete without the other—guarantees you a happy and fulfilling relationship.

**When you understand the divine differences
between you and honor them in that way, you're on track
for tremendous success in marriage.**

CHAPTER 3

Leadership and Submission: God's Perfect Plan for Your Marriage

Now that you understand God's original plan for marriage, you're ready to move on to the next step: How to operate within that plan through leadership and submission.

Yes, *submission*. I know that's not a very popular word these days. In fact, it's a word that has struck fear into the heart of many a woman. Yet it *is* a scriptural word—one that you must understand if the power of God is ever going to flow in your marriage.

The doctrine of submission is one of the most abused doctrines in the Bible. Misguided men have used it as an excuse to oppress and mistreat their wives. They've even twisted it to lead their wives into sin.

But in this chapter, I want to set the record straight. I want to let both husbands and wives know that real, biblical submission is good news, not bad news. It's a principle which, if properly understood, will turn your marriage into the powerhouse God designed it to be.

In Ephesians 5:22-24 the Word of God paints a beautiful picture of a right relationship between man and woman. It is in this picture that the word "submission" appears:

"Wives, submit yourselves unto your own husbands as unto the Lord. For the husband is the head of the wife, even as Christ is the head of the church...Therefore as the church is subject unto Christ, so let the wives be to their own husbands in everything."

The Buck Stops Here

Before we go any further, I want to make something clear. When God designated the husband as the head of the wife, all He did was assign leadership responsibility. Nothing more. He did not indicate that the man is more important than the woman...or smarter than the woman...or any such thing. As a matter of fact, God says that in Christ "there is neither male nor female: for ye are all one in Christ Jesus" (Galatians 3:28).

When you have more than one person involved in anything, one individual has to be assigned final decision-making responsibility or there is anarchy. The buck has to stop with someone—and in the marriage relationship that someone is the man.

Now guys, that doesn't mean God is giving you a little kingship where you can order your wife around and do whatever you want. No, it means He has given you a solemn responsibility to be the leader of your home. What's more, He is expecting you to pattern that leadership after the ministry of Jesus Christ Himself. He says: "Husbands, love your wives, *even as Christ also loved the church, and gave himself for it*" (Ephesians 5:25).

No Bullies Allowed

One of the most outstanding aspects of the leadership of Jesus was that He never forced it on anyone. Everyone who submitted to Him did so voluntarily. True submission in marriage cannot be forced either. Any bully who tries will find one of two things on their hands—bondage or rebellion.

I can just hear you husbands thinking. "Oh great! How do I get my wife to submit to me then?"

By loving her as Christ loved the Church. We are able to love Jesus because we're confident of His love for us. He made the ultimate sacrifice for us. He didn't withhold anything.

Husband, when your wife is that confident in your love for her, when she knows you would lay down your life for her, submission will never be an issue in your family. It will simply be a fact founded on love.

You see, woman in her most basic state was made to respond to man's leadership. She is most comfortable when her man is operating as he's supposed to and she can adapt to the direction God brings the family through him. She *wants* to be in submission!

Why then are so many wives running the show? More often than not, it's because they're having to fill a leadership void left by their husbands.

Me, a Prophet?

To learn how to fill that leadership void we must look back at our pattern—Jesus. His ministry involved three different phases: prophet, priest and king. To follow His example, you as a husband need to minister to your family in the same three ways.

First, there is the prophet role. What does a prophet do? He proclaims the Word of the Lord. As prophet in your home, husband, it's your responsibility to proclaim the Word to your family.

That means taking the initiative and doing it, even if you feel your wife is more spiritual than you. You may find a hundred other excuses not to assume the role of prophet, but unless you're speaking the Word to your family, you've abdicated one of your primary responsibilities as leader.

How do you function as a prophet in your home? There are lots of ways.

It may mean initiating morning or evening family devotions. It could involve something as simple as getting your family to church to hear the anointed Word.

When your child falls and hurts her knee, instead of running for the aspirin and bandages, you speak what God's Word says about healing to her and pray the prayer of faith.

When you're staring at a stack of bills that you don't know how you're going to pay, you don't moan and fret. You proclaim that

God meets all your family's needs according to His riches in glory. You proclaim your deliverance from the curse of poverty.

I realize you may feel strange doing such things at first. But forge ahead anyway. That's what I had to do. I remember not long after I had promised the Lord I would take my role as prophet in my home, my oldest boy, Jim, hurt himself during a ballgame. When it happened, I knew I was going to have to go out there and pray for him. And to tell you the truth, I didn't want to do it.

I didn't even know how to pray very well back then. What's more, many of my old buddies were watching. But even though I felt awkward, I walked onto the field and prayed for Jim. God honored that little step of faith and enabled him to play the rest of the game.

He'll do the same kind of thing for you. Don't worry about your inadequacies. Just take the first step and God will do the rest.

Priest and King

The second aspect of the husband's responsibility as leader in the home is the role of priest.

Jesus, our High Priest, is sitting at the right hand of the Father. There, He is involved in two priestly activities—He intercedes or prays for us, and He ministers to us. Those two priestly functions are the husband's as well.

Husband, it is your responsibility to pray for your family. And I'm not talking about a weak, "Bless my family, Lord," before you fall asleep at night. I'm talking about genuine, serious intercession. The kind of prayer that pleads the blood of Jesus over your wife and children, commissions angels to surround them with protection and keeps them from the snares of the devil.

Wives, this isn't to say that you shouldn't pray as well. It's vital that you do so. It's just that the husband has been given ultimate responsibility and accountability for operating as the priest of the home. We're simply talking about leadership here.

A priest also ministers to his family. When your wife is hurting, you are to minister to her in the power of the Holy Spirit. If your children are experiencing a traumatic situation in school, as the priest of the home you extend the love of God to them and encourage them in the Word.

Operating as a priest by praying and ministering in love is not just an option for a Christian husband who wants to be the kind of leader that Jesus is. It's a *must.*

The final aspect of Jesus' method of leadership is His kingly ministry. It's also the most frequently abused when applied to the marriage relationship.

Husbands, as king in your home, you're responsible to seek God about the direction for your family and carry out that direction in a way that will keep all of you on the course God has planned.

Now, don't take that to mean you simply sit on your throne, make all the decisions, and ignore what your wife has to say. Oh, no. You need to sit down with her and say, "Honey, I feel the Lord is speaking to me about our finances right now..." Then ask her what she thinks.

Why? Because you can't effectively lead without her help. Remember, you two are one flesh (Ephesians 5:31). You are incomplete without her. You need her input, her wisdom and her sensitivity to the Lord to help keep you on track.

Your wife is your best source of counsel. So, seek out her agreement. It's the best safety net God has given you. If you and your wife will agree before making a decision, you're sure to avoid some very costly mistakes.

When you're facing an important decision and you just can't seem to agree—pray together until God changes one of your hearts. Believe me, it's worth the time it takes. You are God's unbeatable team when you move in the power of agreement!

There's That Word Again

If you're a wife, you're probably feeling terrific right now. "You tell him, Pastor Mac!" you're thinking. "Get that man of mine in line."

But wait! There are some things you need to do too. It is a fact that your husband has ultimate responsibility for the success or failure of your family. The buck does stop with him. However, it is also a fact that you can enhance his chances of success many fold. You can make it a whole lot easier for him or you can make it a whole lot harder.

With that in mind, let's go back to that first scripture we read in Ephesians: "Wives, submit yourselves unto your husbands as unto the Lord."

Once again, we're back to that dirty word "submit." Before you jump and run, let me tell you something about submission. It is an attitude not an action. It is not blind obedience. It is an attitude of heart that says, "Yes, I see that I need to receive godly direction through this authority God has set in place in my life."

Notice I said you needed to receive "godly" direction. How then should you respond to your husband if he isn't walking with God? How do you deal with ungodly leadership?

First Peter, chapter 3 gives the answer. "Likewise, ye wives, be in subjection to your own husbands; that, if any obey not the word, they also may without the word be won by the conversation (or manner of life) of the wives; while they behold your chaste conversation (manner of life) coupled with fear (or reverence)."

Preach with Your Life—Not Your Lips

This is good news, dear lady! You don't have to say a word to that ungodly husband. In fact, the Bible is telling you not to. So how *do* you win him over?

Two ways. First, by your chaste manner of life. (Chaste means pure, separated unto God.) And second, by your reverence. Reverence of who? Of your husband!

The Amplified Bible makes that very clear. It says you are to conduct yourself with reverence "[for your husband. That is, you are to feel for him all that reverence includes]—to respect, defer to, revere him;...to honor, esteem (appreciate, prize), and [in the human sense] adore him;...to admire, praise, be devoted to, deeply love and enjoy [your husband]" (verse 2).

"Oh, but you don't know what a cantankerous man my husband is!" you may be saying.

It doesn't matter. This is what God says you're to do. God doesn't call you to do something without equipping you. That means by the power of the Holy Spirit, you can do it! And when you do, it will change the direction of your husband's life.

It is important to remember however, that submission to an ungodly man doesn't mean obedience. You are to receive whatever godly direction comes through him. But if he says, "Woman, you submit. Skip church and go to the bar with me today," don't you do it. You obey God instead.

God says you're to live a chaste life, holy, pure and separated to Him. So, just gently, lovingly kiss your husband on the cheek and say, "I'm going to church, Honey. Bye."

Through it all, continue to do what the Word says. Be loving. Be kind to him. Encourage him. Adore him as your husband. Build him up and pray for him and he will change. Eventually, the day will come when he wakes you up and says, "Hurry up and get dressed or we'll be late for church!" Eventually, *he'll* be the one living the Word in front of *you.*

Miracles happen in marriage. Husbands, they'll happen for you if you'll love and minister to your wife like Jesus does. Wives, they'll happen for you if you'll live a godly life and reverence your husband.

Adapt your lives to the pattern you see
in the Word of God and your marriage will be glorious. It will
turn your home into a spiritual powerhouse!

CHAPTER 4

Mastering the Uncommon Art of Communication

The great communicator. That's what the media dubbed former President Ronald Reagan. He had such a way with words, such an ability to speak gently and still make a strong point that even the news reporters who criticized him couldn't help but like him.

Are you a great communicator?

If you're not, you'd better become one. Because nothing has a greater impact on your marriage than your ability to communicate effectively with your spouse. If you don't communicate well, your marriage is not going to be everything God intended it to be.

Some of you husbands especially may be groaning in despair right now. "I guess it's all over then," you say. "I've never been any good at talking and I never will be."

That's not true! Even if communicating doesn't come naturally to you, you still have the capacity not just do it, but to do it well! Every one of us has that capacity. All we have to do is follow the instructions God has given us in His Word.

Pass the Salt, Please

God sets high standards for our communication. He makes that quite clear in Colossians 4:6: "Let your speech be always with grace, seasoned with salt, that ye may know how ye ought to answer every man."

Stop for a moment and read that verse again. How often does it tell us to season our speech with the salt of grace? Always. Not occasionally. Not just when your spouse deserves it. Not just on special occasions. ALWAYS.

That challenge is reaffirmed in Ephesians 4:29: "Let no corrupt communication proceed out of your mouth, but that which is good to the use of edifying, that it may minister grace unto the hearers."

No corrupt communication. *Only* that which is good to the use of edifying. *Only* the things that minister grace to the hearers.

"Isn't that a pretty tall order?" Yes! But fulfill it and your marriage will work wonderfully, ignore it and your marriage will suffer. That's the simple truth.

If you think I'm overstating the importance of speech and communication, take a look at the Greek word the New Testament uses for them—*logos.*

Can you think of another passage of scripture where the *logos* figures prominently? John 1: "In the beginning was the Word *[logos]*, and the Word *[logos]* was with God, and the Word *[logos]* was God."

Communication is so important that God named Jesus "Communication." Think about that! Jesus, the living Word, is God's communication to mankind. And just as God communicates to us through Jesus, we should communicate Jesus to one another.

Everything you say to your spouse should in some way reveal the character of Jesus. All your communication should demonstrate the peace, the love, the joy, the gentleness, the kindness, the power and the authority that's in Him.

That sounds great, doesn't it? But let's get real. It is one thing to preach the principles of communication, it is another thing to live by them. So let's look at some keys you can use to put these principles into practice on a day-to-day basis.

Offend Not!

The most important principle of effective communication is: **Avoid Offending Your Listener.**

Real communication requires an atmosphere of trust and support. When you put your listener on the defensive, when you make him feel threatened, you destroy that atmosphere and he cannot accurately hear what you say. *Defensiveness distorts the listener's interpretation of your words.*

Secular researchers who've explored the subject of communication are in almost total agreement on this issue. The single greatest deterrent to effective communication is an atmosphere in which one party feels threatened and the need to defend themselves.

James 3:2 tells us, "For in many things we offend all. If any man *offend not in word,* the same is a perfect [mature] man, and able also to *bridle* the whole body." Now that word bridle very simply means to guide. And it's not only referring to your own physical body, it is also referring to the part of the Body of Christ that you contact with your communication.

In other words, you can communicate direction to your fellow believers, speak your heart to them and bring guidance to their lives if you're able to speak without offending. This point is especially important to remember when it comes to husbands and wives because we're so vulnerable to each other. We know each other's weaknesses, shortcomings and sensitivities. The potential for threat there is much greater.

That's why it's doubly important that you "offend not in word" when it comes to talking with your spouse.

If you can come to the place in your marriage where you speak without causing your spouse to be offended or feel threatened you will have set the stage for true communication to take place. Here are three scriptural keys to help you along.

Be Swift to Hear

The first key to non-threatening communication is this: **Be Quick to Listen and Slow to Speak.**

James 1:19 says, "Wherefore, my beloved brethren, let every man be swift to hear, slow to speak, slow to wrath...." However, most of the husbands and wives I've had to counsel over the years are exactly the opposite. They are slow to hear, swift to speak and extremely swift to get angry.

In the minds of many people, "listening" is so far down the list of priorities, they don't even think of it when the word communication is mentioned! All they think about is talking. But in reality, listening is the most important part.

Listening has a powerfully positive impact on your partner. More than anything else you can do or say, listening demonstrates that you care. Listening says, "Your feelings are important to me. I care about your viewpoint. I care enough to hear what you have to say."

When your partner knows you care, the defenses come down and real communication can begin.

Say Something Positive

Once you've listened to your spouse, you'll be ready to use the second key to non-threatening communication: **Make Your First Response Positive.**

Proverbs 16:24 tells us, "Pleasant words are as an honeycomb, sweet to the soul, and health to the bones." When you've listened to your spouse—when you've heard him or her out—make the first words you speak "pleasant words." They will establish an atmosphere that is sweet to your partner's soul (mind, will and emotions).

"But you haven't heard how my wife talks to me!" you may be saying to yourself. "It's hard to think of anything pleasant to say when I get through listening to her."

Then just keep listening until you can. Try to hear beyond what the emotional words are saying and discern the "why" behind them. Listen for the real motivating factors. If you have to, encourage your spouse to keep talking until you can respond positively to what's really on her heart.

Even when someone gives you a real tongue lashing—make your first answer positive and soft. That's not only scriptural, it's just plain smart. Why?

Because, "A soft answer turneth away wrath..." (Proverbs 15:1). I've seen that principle work time and again. It's like popping a balloon. Soft words deflate anger and if you'll speak them every time an argument starts, most of those arguments won't last more than two seconds.

Please understand me now. I am not saying you should just let your spouse verbally walk all over you. I'm not saying that at all. It's possible to take a strong stand and refuse to let yourself be abused without being harsh or belligerent. State your position firmly. Just be sure to be gentle at the same time.

When you do, you'll find that you've begun to create an atmosphere of trust and caring—an atmosphere in which your spouse feels free to share his or her heart.

Dare to Admit You're Wrong

All of us like to think we're right. We like to prove our point and win the argument. That's human nature. But if you're going to use the final key to non-threatening communication, you'll have to set that tendency aside and: **Be Willing to Yield When You are Wrong.**

James 3:17 says, "...the wisdom that is from above is first pure, then peaceable, gentle, and easy to be entreated...." Or as *The Amplified Bible* says, "...[It is willing to] yield to reason...."

One of the essential ingredients to producing the right kind of atmosphere for effective communication is a willingness to say, "I blew it." It builds trust in your marriage partner. When they realize that, rather than being unreasonable in your position, you're going to be "peaceable, gentle, and easy to be entreated," those walls of defensiveness will come tumbling down.

Give up the need to always be right. I've known far too many people who "won" their arguments and ended up losing something much more precious.

Study the Master

If you're going to "offend not," you must (1) Be swift to hear, (2) Say something positive and (3) Dare to admit you're wrong. Just those three keys will take you a long way toward good communication. But if you want to be a truly great communicator, you'll need to open the Word and study the Master.

Study the life and Words of Jesus. With all due respect to former President Reagan, Jesus is the real Great Communicator. He's our model.

So take the time to learn from Him.
Then make a commitment to put what you learn into action. Make communication a priority in your marriage and you'll fall in love all over again.

CHAPTER 5

My Needs/Your Needs I: The Two-Sided Secret of a Satisfying Marriage

"My needs aren't being met!" Once you and your spouse really start listening to each other, that is probably what you're going to hear. It's the battle cry of 99 percent of the people who come to me for marriage counseling.

Physical needs. Spiritual needs. Emotional and intellectual needs. Men and women both have them. God designed us that way.

In fact, if you remember what we learned in Chapter 2 about the creation of man and woman, you know just where those markedly differing needs came from.

God initially created Man perfect and whole with all of the components of both the male and female personalities housed in one body of flesh called Adam. When God took woman out of man, it left gaps in each of them. Each became incomplete without the other.

Thus, ever since the Garden of Eden, men and women have needed each other. And when they come together in marriage, according to God's plan, those needs are met.

At least, they are *supposed* to be met. In reality, what often happens is that men and women fail to realize just how strikingly different each other's needs really are. As a result, neither the husband nor the wife are fulfilled...and trouble follows.

If their needs continue to go unrecognized and unmet, the collapse of the marriage is almost unavoidable. I know. I see it all too frequently.

Become Need-Conscious

That's why I want to challenge you to start being more need-conscious. That's right. You need to be more need-conscious. No, I'm not talking about being aware of your own needs. I'm talking about developing a greater understanding of the needs of your spouse.

Such an understanding can save a failing marriage. It can make a good one even stronger. It will end up blessing you as much as it blesses your partner.

Most people don't understand that. They think, "My wife has certain needs and I have certain needs." They separate out "his needs" and "her needs." But the truth is, they are all a part of "the relationship's needs."

You and your spouse are one flesh, the Bible says. What enriches one of you enriches the other as well.

This is what the Spirit of God is telling us in Ephesians 5:28-29: "So ought men to love their wives as their own bodies. *He that loveth his wife loveth himself.* For no man ever yet hated his own flesh; but nourisheth it and cherisheth it, even as the Lord the Church...."

In other words, God is saying, "Listen folks, when you do something for your spouse, you're doing it for yourself! It's just like ministering to your own body. Husbands, when you meet a need in your wife's life, you're meeting it in your own life."

Now up to this point, I've primarily been talking about the spiritual aspects of marriage. But the truth is, you and I are three-part beings. Not only are we spirit, but we also have a soul (our mind, will and emotions), and we live in a body.

God created us with needs in each of these areas. We can't afford to focus so much on the spiritual side of things that we ignore the God-given needs of our soul and body. Our needs in those areas must be met too if our marriages are going to work the way God intends.

What are the most important of those needs?

The answer depends on whether you're a man or a woman. Wives and husbands have differing needs. That fact is confirmed not only by the Bible but by secular studies and research as well. (Note: Don't automatically dismiss information just because it comes from the world. Secular researchers often uncover truth when they unknowingly stumble across scriptural principles.)

Nearly all the studies I've seen in this area report that everyone has 10 or 12 basic needs. Yet the top five needs for women are very different from the top five for men. In the next few chapters we're going to find out what those needs are and discover some ways to meet them.

On practically all of the lists of needs that have been compiled, one particular need consistently shows up as being the most intense for men. A different need area almost always shows up as being most important for women. Would you like to know what your spouse's "Number One" need is?

The "S" Word

It may come as no surprise to you that the number one need for men is for sexual fulfillment.

No doubt, some men reading this right now are thinking, "Wait a minute, that's not true for me!" But those men are the exception, not the rule. In the overwhelming number of cases, sexual fulfillment is a man's primary need in a marriage relationship.

That isn't to say that the wife has no need for physical fulfillment, because she does. It is simply farther down on her list of priorities.

I see evidence of just how vital the physical part of the marriage relationship actually is to men almost every time a couple with marriage problems walks into my office for counseling. The man's unfulfilled sexual needs are a trouble-making issue in nearly every case. That trouble can take many forms—extreme irritability and belligerence on the part of the husband, for one. He may not even be aware of it, but the sexual frustration he feels can produce resentment toward the wife.

Another even more disastrous result of a husband's sexual needs going unmet is that it can lead to his involvement in sexual fantasy. On the surface this may seem like a harmless activity. It's not. Fantasy will invariably lead to adultery. Why? "As a man thinketh in his heart, so is he."

No wonder God's Word says in 1 Corinthians 7:4-5: "The wife hath not power of her own body, but the husband: and likewise also the husband hath not power of his own body, but the wife. Defraud ye not one the other, except it be with consent for a time, that ye may give yourselves to fasting and prayer...."

This verse is the only place in all of Scripture where God makes meeting the needs of another person an absolute mandate. He is saying, "This is so important that you don't have an option. When you're not meeting that need for your spouse, you have defrauded him or her."

I realize the subject of sex very rarely is discussed in Christian circles. It has generally been a taboo subject. That's probably one reason the devil has been having such a field day in this area. We haven't been shining the light of God's Word on it. But it's time we changed that. It's time we began viewing sex in light of God's plan.

One reason the devil works overtime to mess things up in this area is that, in marriage, the sex act is the literal physical manifestation of two becoming "one flesh." Of course the spiritual aspect of becoming one flesh is important. But so is the physical outworking of that spiritual reality.

Wives, you need to understand that when your husband expresses to you his need for sexual fulfillment, he's not being carnal or worldly. He's expressing something God put within him.

One of God's commands to Adam was to "be fruitful and multiply and fill the earth." A man's sexual needs make up the drive that compels him to bring eternal life into existence.

It's an awesome thing when you think about it. We are the only beings other than God Himself who can create eternal life. When a child is conceived, an eternal being who never existed before comes into existence. That child will live forever, either in heaven or in hell.

Ladies, once you begin to see your husband's desire as a God-given and vitally important part of the divine plan of creation and honor it as such, your marriage will take a giant step forward.

What Wives Really Want

Now that you know the number one need in husbands, would you like to know what the researchers say is the number one need for wives?

Affection.

That's right, husbands. Just as strong as your need for sexual fulfillment is your wife's need for affection. She has a very real, very powerful hunger for it.

Once again, in this area researchers have stumbled upon a biblical truth. Every study I've seen confirms that, as a rule, the wife's primary need is for affection. Guess what. It's been in the Word all along!

Remember when we looked at Ephesians 5:28? It instructed husbands to "nourish and cherish" their wives as they would their own flesh. Nothing makes a wife feel as nourished and cherished as a husband's display of affection.

Why then are so few men given to those kinds of displays? It's because the world has brainwashed them into thinking it's un-manly to show affection. The world says that a "real" man is hard, unfeeling and independent. I can assure you, the devil is working overtime to promote that image.

I fell for that lie myself when I was younger. I remember one incident back when I was a pilot in training. My wife, Lynne, and I had only been married a few months. One day we were grocery shopping. As we walked along we were holding hands and being very sweet and affectionate.

Then I looked down an aisle and saw two of my pilot buddies walking toward us. Immediately I started trying to wriggle my hand out of Lynne's. But the more I tried to get loose, the tighter she hung onto me. We ended up looking like we were arm wrestling!

Of course, now I realize how foolish that was. I also understand the kind of message that must have sent to my wife.

Husbands, you have to get rid of the idea that affection is somehow unmanly. Your marriage depends on it. You've got to learn to show her affection whether you feel like it at that moment or not.

She needs affection as much as you need the physical fulfillment of the marriage bed. But don't confuse her need for affection with your need for sex. All too often a woman's expression of a need to be held will be misinterpreted as a signal to initiate sex. She simply wants to feel close to him and he thinks it's time to head for the bedroom. The result is that her need for affection goes unmet.

When this happens consistently, she can begin to feel frustrated and resentful. Often she will stop giving herself freely to her husband in the marriage bed. Then he begins to get frustrated because his sexual needs aren't being met. It's a destructive downward spiral.

Husbands, you need to realize how important this need is to your wife. It's not silly. She's not being unreasonable. She's expressing a God-given need of the relationship.

"But I'm just not an affectionate person. I don't know how."

If you don't know how to express affection, here are a few practical suggestions to help you get started.

The simplest way to show your wife affection is to hug her and give her a little kiss every so often. Do it without any sexual overtones or expectations. Just do it to show her you love her.

Hold her hand. Whisper sweet nothings in her ear. Tell her how pretty you think she is. Send her flowers every now and then. But don't stop there. Get creative! There are a thousand different ways to let your wife know that she's your one-and-only.

When all is said and done, what's important is not the methods you use to express your affection, but the fact that you genuinely let your wife know that you're blessed by her—that you're proud of her, that she's the crowning joy of your life and you're never going to forget it.

If you'll do that, I can guarantee that you'll never have any problems with sexual fulfillment. The two things go hand-in-hand.

My needs, your needs. They're very different but equally important. As you both unselfishly meet each other's needs, you'll be strengthening the relationship. Even better, you'll be developing the kind of tightly bonded, one-flesh marriage that will make you "heirs together of the grace of life."

CHAPTER 6

My Needs/Your Needs II: "Talk to me you big, handsome man!"

Many centuries have passed since God introduced Male to Female in the Garden of Eden. You'd think they would have figured each other out by now.

But even after thousands of years of living together, men and women are still a mystery to each other. And the depth of that mystery is most evident when they start trying to understand and meet one another's needs in marriage.

In the previous chapter we took a step toward solving this mystery. We discovered the first and most important marital need for husbands (sex) and wives (affection). Now let's take another step toward solving the marriage-mystery by exploring need number two.

Can We Talk?

Let's start with the ladies. Researchers agree their second most important need is the need for conversation. That's right, husbands, *conversation!* (Yes, I know we already spent an entire chapter discussing the subject of communication but it's so important, we're going to examine it again.)

Many jokes have been made about how a woman can talk and talk and talk...but those jokes have a basis in fact. A woman's need to talk is much greater than a man's. And, fellow, it isn't a joke any more than your need for sex is a joke.

When I say a woman needs to talk, I don't mean she just likes to chatter. She needs the real, sharing kind of conversation. She needs her husband to be interested in what happened to her today...and where she went...and who she saw.

Many guys don't understand this need. So when their wife comes in and says, "Let's talk, honey," they glance up from the newspaper and say, "Okay. What do you want to talk about?"

Husbands, please don't ever do that! Why? Because you're actually implying that she isn't interesting enough to you to cause you to want to have a conversation, but you'll be patient with her while she talks. You've insulted her! Let me turn the tables and put it in terms you understand a little more. Let's say you walked into the room and said, "Honey, let's have sex." And she glances over the newspaper and says, "What for, George? Is it time to have kids again?"

You may think those two situations are different, but they're not. Your wife needs to talk as much as you need to be sexually fulfilled. So recognize that need. Quit conforming to the worldly image of the strong, silent type who just grunts once in a while and be diligent to share your heart with her.

Notice I said, be *diligent.* You'll have to deliberately set time aside for communication or it won't take place. How much time should you allot? Most psychologists agree that 15 hours a week or so is really what's needed—say, about an hour a day during the week and the rest on the weekends.

I can just hear some of you guys right now. "Fifteen hours! I can't spend 15 hours a week talking to my wife!" Yes, you can. Not by sitting in two chairs staring at each other for hours on end—but by planning activities together. Go walking or bike riding. Do things you enjoy and talk while you're at it.

Time spent in front of the television does not count. Neither does the time when the kids are harassing you and you're being distracted by a myriad of other things. Pick a time during the day when you can give one another your attention. Then, let the conversation flow. You—yes, even you, Strong Silent Husband—may end up enjoying it more than you think.

My Hero!

The number two need husbands most frequently mention may surprise you. It's admiration. That's right, ladies. Your husband has a very real need to know you admire him. God points to the importance of this need in Ephesians 5:33b: "...and [let] the wife see that she respects and reverences her husband—that she notices him, regards him, honors him, prefers him, venerates him and esteems him; and that she defers to him, praises him, and loves and *admires* him exceedingly" (*The Amplified Bible*).

That's quite a mouthful isn't it?

The reason God puts such an emphasis on this is because it is so vitally important to a man. He needs admiration to function properly as the mighty spiritual warrior God created him to be.

Have you ever noticed the way little boys will show off for little girls? If so, you know this need to be admired surfaces early and continues right on into adolescence as teenage boys go to great lengths to impress any girl who happens to be watching. Some women simply think such attempts at admiration-evoking are just a male "pride thing." But they're wrong. The need for admiration is a God-designed facet of the male ego. And that ego, when properly fueled, will propel and energize a man to do the things God has called him to do.

Be assured, ladies, nothing will light your man's fire any faster than to have you, the woman he loves, tell him how great he is and that he's your knight in shining armor. When that happens, he'll be ready to conquer the world. When it doesn't happen, he'll become a target for the devil.

You see, this is an area that is frequently exploited by Satan to get men involved in extramarital affairs. If a man is getting nothing but criticism at home and then goes to the office where some pretty little secretary treats him like he's superman, he's ripe for the picking.

Remember that and don't let the enemy deceive you into focusing on what is wrong with your man. Don't let him magnify those faults until they're all you can see. Instead, choose to begin focusing on admiring those things that are right.

A word of warning is in order here, ladies. Although it is vital you express your admiration for your husband, don't ever make empty, flattering comments. He will detect the insincerity of them and they will drive a wedge between you.

Be genuine! Let the admiration emanate from your heart. If you have a hard time finding qualities you admire about your husband right now, then ask the Holy Spirit to show you some. They may be hard to see right now, but they're there.

I know a lady, for example, who absolutely hated the fact that her husband was so hardheaded. He wouldn't listen to anything anybody had to say. Then one day the Spirit of the Lord showed her that what appeared to be hardheadedness would actually become determination once he received direction from the Lord.

From then on, that wife saw her husband in a whole new light. She recognized the gift of God in him and it enabled her to admire something very important about him.

God will do the same thing for you if you'll trust Him to reveal things to you about your husband. I promise you, you'll be amazed at the wonderful qualities you'll find.

CHAPTER 7

My Needs/ Your Needs III: A Lot of Truth... and a Little Makeup

Honest to Goodness

Would you like to know what the third most important need is for most wives? Good old-fashioned honesty and openness.

Naturally, both husbands *and* wives need to be honest with each other, but this is an acute need for women. Every wife needs to know the man who shares her life is always being honest with her.

This is especially vital because it affects a woman's response to a man's authority and headship in the home. Husbands, if your wife is going to be able to respond to your authority and leadership, she needs to know she can trust you. If she senses you're not being completely honest with her or that you're hiding something from her, she won't be able to properly submit to your leadership.

Take a look at 1 John 1:6-7: "If we say that we have fellowship with him, and walk in darkness, we lie, and do not know the truth: But if we walk in the light, as he is in the light, we have fellowship one with another, and the blood of Jesus Christ his Son cleanseth us from all sin."

Light is a symbol for the Word of God. You need to walk with your wife in the "light" of the Word. But "light" also means to have everything open and visible—no subterfuge, no deception. Only when we are walking in that kind of light can we have right fellowship with one another.

Obviously the single greatest obstacle to walking in the "light" with your wife is the practice of lying. Of course, husbands don't have a monopoly on lying, wives do it too. But as the person in the position of leadership, it's especially important that the husband eliminate this harmful habit from their lives.

When a husband lies to his wife, it is usually for one of three reasons:

1) He is a chronic or habitual liar. This usually stems from some type of self-esteem problem. This person feels that he needs to put himself in a better light by improving on the truth. This usually begins in early childhood and continues as a life-habit or stronghold right on into adulthood.

We all know people like that. It can be very troubling to be married to one of them.

If you've been a chronic liar in the past, I have good news for you. When you were born again that old man passed away. You're a new creature, so start acting like it. Stop lying.

2) He lies to avoid conflict. Here's an example.

Suppose Lynne calls me at work and asks me to stop by the store on the way home and pick up a few things, but I forget to do it. When I walk in the front door, she asks, "Did you go to the store?" If I say, "Uhhh, yeah...I did, but they were out of what you wanted," I've just lied to avoid conflict.

What usually happens when this type of lying consistently take place? The wife eventually catches on and comes to believe that her husband is not trustworthy.

3) He lies to protect his wife.

On the surface this type of lying looks sort of noble—even chivalrous. It's not. This guy tries to "protect" his wife by not telling her how bad a given situation is.

He tells her things are fine when the family is in serious financial trouble. She doesn't know anything is wrong until someone shows up at the door to foreclose on the house. This type of lying is very unfair and just plain stupid.

There is no room in the marriage relationship for dishonesty of any type. Dishonesty breeds distrust. Where there is distrust there can be no true fellowship.

Men, you must be truthful with your wife. She needs it. And as your God-given partner, she deserves it.

Pretty is Good!

The husband's number three need is his need to feel that his wife is attractive. Most every man in the world wants other people to look at his wife and say, "Wow, he certainly is blessed to be married to *her!*"

Now this may sound like bad news to some of you ladies. You may be saying, "Hey, aren't Christians supposed to be looking beyond the outward man and into the inner person?"

Yes, but the scripture most frequently cited to support the position that Christians shouldn't be concerned about their outward appearance has been misunderstood by most people.

The passage I'm referring to is 1 Peter 3:3 where the Holy Spirit, through Peter, is instructing wives how to win their husbands.

"Whose adorning let it not be that outward adorning of plaiting the hair, and of wearing of gold, or of putting on of apparel; But let it be the hidden man of the heart, in that which is not corruptible, even the ornament of a meek and quiet spirit, which is in the sight of God of great price."

Many people misinterpret this verse because the *King James Version* makes it a little unclear. *The Amplified Bible* more accurately says, "Let not yours be the *[merely]* external adorning..." and the *New American Standard* says, "...let not your adornment be merely external...."

Ladies, God isn't against your making yourself look good. In fact, He's for it! He's just saying don't stop there—go further and make sure you've taken care of the inside too.

Some women use this verse as an excuse to totally let themselves go, physically. I see it quite often as a pastor and marriage counselor. A woman will get married, have a baby and begin to allow her appearance to slide downhill. She won't pay much attention to her weight anymore. She'll get so busy chasing the kids that she won't bother with her hair or put on much makeup. Often the husband of such a woman will profess to not care about his wife's appearance. But deep down inside he usually does.

Women tend to be more spiritually sensitive than men. And men tend to be moved more easily by their senses, particularly their sense of sight. Wives, that means you can actually minister to your husband by taking care of yourself outwardly. You can use that as a way to say, "Honey, I love you so much I want to bless you by looking my best." It will endear you to him more than 99 percent of the other things you can do.

I'm not suggesting that if you're not magazine cover-girl material your husband is dissatisfied. I am saying that you should make every effort to look your personal best. I firmly believe an attractive woman is made, not born. With proper nutrition and diet you can shake those extra pounds. You can find a flattering hairstyle. Dress yourself up. Put on a little makeup. There's nothing wrong with that. I mean, if you can use it to cover up a few spots and blemishes before Jesus returns, do it!

I guarantee it will make an impact on your husband. It will bless him and make your marriage stronger.

CHAPTER 8

My Needs/ Your Needs IV: A Matter of Domestic (and Financial) Security

Bringing Home the Bacon

Okay, men, now it's your turn again. Would you like to know what comes in at number four on most wives' list of needs? It's financial security. That's no big surprise, really. You knew it had to be in there somewhere, didn't you?

Yes, your wife has a very real, legitimate need to know that the family's needs are going to be met.

All the needs we've examined to this point have had a basis in scripture and this one is no exception. Look at 1 Timothy 5:8: "But if any provide not for his own, and specially for those of his own house, he hath denied the faith, and is worse than an infidel."

That's mighty heavy stuff, guys. God's Word makes it clear that it is your solemn, God-given responsibility to make sure that your family is financially secure. I believe that means your wife shouldn't *have* to work if she doesn't want to.

Many problems in our society today can be traced to women having to work to help make ends meet. Notice I said *having* to work. It's the source of many marriage problems as well. Why? Because when a wife is forced to work outside the home for financial reasons, she faces potential resentment toward her husband.

So what are the alternatives to the wife working outside the home when the bills aren't getting paid? Well, praise God, there are some natural, physical steps you can take and, if you're a Christian, there are also some powerful supernatural steps you can take as well.

In the spiritual realm God has provided a way of prospering and increasing called "planting seed." We can tithe and give offerings and then watch God supernaturally work in our financial lives.

From the natural perspective, you have three basic options when your income isn't meeting your outgo. First, the husband can work a second job or longer hours. Second, the wife can go to work outside the home and supplement the family's income.

Third, and I believe wisest of the three options, is to reduce the family's standard of living to meet its current income. God has given you a certain number of dollars each month and He expects you to be a good steward and live within those means.

To do that, you're going to have to have a *budget*. No, that's not a dirty word. It's something that will help you locate all the holes in your pockets so you can plug them up. If you plug those holes and still find you're struggling to get by, husbands, you may need to take some steps to increase your income potential. You may need to change jobs or vocations.

You may even need to go back to college for a year or two. In that case, you might want to go to your wife and say, "Honey, for us to live comfortably, I am going to have to earn more money. In order to do that, I want to go back to school and get some training. Would you consider working and generating some extra income while I do?"

Chances are, your wife is not going to resent that kind of arrangement because you're giving her a choice. The problems come when she's *forced* to work.

There are a lot of good books on personal finance currently available in Christian bookstores. Any number of them will give more detailed steps on making your income meet your "outgo."

Regardless of what steps you have to take, realize this, husbands. It is your responsibility to provide for your family. If you'll ask God to show you how, He will. He'll open the doors of opportunity to you, and then as you become faithful in doing those things, more opportunities to prosper will arise.

Home Sweet Home

Just as most wives have a genuine need for financial security, most husbands have a strong need for *domestic* security. That is the number four need on his top-five list.

What do I mean by "domestic security?" Domestic security describes a man's need to know things are being cared for at home while he's out hammering away winning the bread. He needs to be assured that when he comes home his house is going to be in order.

Many wives don't fully appreciate or understand what it means to a man to know the homefront is being taken care of while he's out doing his best to earn a living. First Timothy 5:14 speaks of this need: "I will therefore that the younger women marry, bear children, *guide the house*, give none occasion to the adversary to speak reproachfully."

To a man, a well-ordered home is a refuge. Having that type of refuge from the stresses and pressures of the outside world meets a very important need in his life.

Before he gets married, a guy often fantasizes about what it's going to be like to have the perfect home. He dreams about coming home in the evening and having his wife meet him at the door. Looking beautiful, she hugs him around the neck and says, "Hello, darling." Then all his children gather around him and say, "Welcome home, Daddy!"

Then everyone ushers him into the den and somebody brings him his paper. At dinner time, the family has a wonderful meal with nice, quiet, edifying conversation (no conflicts or confrontations). And afterward, as the sun is setting, they go outside and walk down the road together as a family.

Finally, bedtime comes. The kids go to sleep with a prayer and a kiss. Then husband and wife sit on the porch swing, talking for a while in the cool of the evening. Eventually the whole scene winds up with a passionate night of love-making.

No doubt, you're laughing by now at such an unreal idea of family life. Yet, wives, it's important for you to know about those unrealistic dreams because it will help you set your direction. And, according to the Word, guiding and administrating the home is primarily your responsibility. If the husband is ever going to have any of those hopes realized, you are the one who's going to make it possible.

Naturally, if the wife works outside the home there is going to have to be some type of division of labor around the house. She cannot be expected to shoulder the burden of maintaining the home alone.

But if the wife is a full-time homemaker, she has a God-ordained responsibility to make that home a haven for her husband. In either case, the home needs to be maintained as a refuge—a place of order, security and peace.

I've seen a number of instances in which a Christian homemaker became so involved in "spiritual" things that she let her home go to pieces. She was constantly off at some church function or spiritual activity. Consequently, when the husband got home the house was a wreck, the kids were out of control and nothing had been done.

That's a prescription for trouble, ladies. The fact that the activities taking you away from the home are spiritual in nature, doesn't release you from your responsibility of guiding the home. Biblically, if he's the breadwinner, you're the home manager. That's the deal.

Family and Fun

The last of the top five needs for wives is "family commitment."

Family commitment means the husband has a vital, active interest in everything going on in the family.

The Bible teaches a man's family should be second in priority only to his relationship to God. You can see how much importance God places on family commitment in Genesis 18. There, in effect, God says, "I can bless Abraham because I know he will command and direct his children and his household in My ways."

Every wife needs to know that her husband takes ultimate and final responsibility for everything that concerns the family.

Men, that means sitting down with your wife and discussing the decisions that need to be made; establishing the vision for the family; talking about the discipline and education of the children; and generally taking an active role in the family.

It also means spending real, quality time with the children, as individuals and as a group. I'm not talking about sitting together in front of the television, either. I'm talking about real times of interaction.

The fifth need most frequently cited by husbands is for "recreational companionship."

"What on earth is recreational companionship?" I hear you wives asking.

It simply means getting involved and going along as he pursues some of his interests. The old stereotype of a husband always leaving his wife at home to go have fun with the boys should have no place in a Christian home. His best buddy is to be you.

He shouldn't have to go out with the boys every time he wants to do something fun. Get involved with him. Sit down with him and develop mutual interests. It will meet a very important need in his life and strengthen your relationship like few other things can.

Well, there you have it—the top five needs for husbands and wives. Put them all together and you have the unbreakable, one-flesh relationship that God designed.

As you learn to identify and meet each other's unique needs, you'll find more fulfillment, happiness and joy in your marriage than you ever dreamed possible.

CHAPTER 9

Sailing the Seven "C's" of a Great Relationship

Attitudes...sexual roles...leadership...submission...his needs... her needs—obviously, having a successful, scriptural marriage isn't an instant, or easy, task. But it can be done.

Not by reading a book like this one time—but by putting God's principles to work in your marriage day by day, moment by moment for the rest of your life. To help you do that, I want to leave you with a simple checklist you can remember and use again and again as you face the challenges ahead. I call them the seven "C's" of a great relationship.

1. Communicate

We've been over this several times now. But in case you missed it, let me say one more time: Communication is the basis of any successful relationship. So, if you aren't already a good communicator, become one. Then, deliberately schedule in time for that communication to take place. If you don't, it won't happen and your marriage will suffer.

2. Cover One Another

First Peter 4:8 says, "...above all things have fervent charity among yourselves: for charity shall cover the multitude of sins." If you truly love your spouse, you won't expose, humiliate or condemn them when they make a mistake, you will cover them. Wives, you won't point your finger at your husband and tell how often he fails to pray or how carnal he is much of the time. And husbands, you won't point your finger at your wife and tell how much she nags. No! You'll cover each other's weaknesses.

You'll cover with gentleness even when harshness may seem justified. You'll cover by being patient, even when you want to snap a rebuke. You'll cover by praying for each other, when it would be a whole lot easier to walk out. Cover each other with love.

3. Cherish One Another

Ephesians 5:29 says, "For no man ever yet hated his own flesh; but nourisheth and cherisheth it, even as the Lord the Church." The word *cherish* there literally means *to feel or show affection.* Affection is the outward display of tender emotion one to another. As you may remember, it is the wife's number one need. But, men, it is important for you as well.

You see, affection will give you the emotional impetus you need to continue acting in love even when things are tough. It is the glue that will bond you together in good times and bad. You're not going to be able to give to someone day after day if you don't feel any affection for them. So make it a priority to develop—and display!—affection.

4. Comfort One Another

"Blessed be God, even the Father of our Lord Jesus Christ, the Father of mercies, and the God of all comfort; Who comforteth us in all our tribulation, that we may be able to comfort them which are in any trouble, by the comfort wherewith we ourselves are comforted of God" (2 Corinthians 1:3).

Comfort is a vitally important element that enables us to stand successfully against the devil in every area of our lives. It makes it easier for us to be patient. For example, imagine a guy who is stuck in traffic. He is late for an appointment but he can't move until the car in front of him moves. His car is in terrible shape. The exhaust is leaking, the windows are rolled down and it's 100 degrees outside. Mosquitoes are all over the place. It is going to be much harder for that fellow to be patient than it will for the fellow behind him who is sitting in an air-conditioned Cadillac with his windows rolled up and a good faith message on the tape player.

You are intended by God to be your spouse's greatest source of comfort. You're the one to bring them tenderness when they're hurt, words of hope when they're discouraged, and companionship when it seems the whole world has forsaken them. If you'll do it, you will go a long way in giving your spouse the staying power he or she needs to win out over the devil in trying times.

5. Compel One Another

Hebrews 10:24-25 instructs us to "consider one another to provoke unto love and to good works...exhorting one another: and so much the more, as ye see the day approaching." Again, just as you're to be the greatest source of comfort to your spouse, you're also to be the one God primarily uses to compel them toward love and good works. You're to be the one who encourages them to greater heights in the Lord. Don't nag. Urge one another. Inspire one another. Keep yourselves from becoming weary in well doing by reminding each other that harvest time is coming! (See Galatians 6:9.)

6. Consult with One Another

Amos 3:3 asks a simple but profound question. "Can two walk together except they be agreed?" The answer is: no! Agreement is a foundational principle of relationship success. Violate that principle and strife will see to it that your marriage will eventually fail. So consult with each other until you can agree.

Remember, when you got married, you married someone who filled your needs. That person is your balance. He or she is God's gift, specifically designed to help keep you from making mistakes. Don't squander that gift!

7. Cleave to One Another

"Therefore shall a man leave his father and his mother, and shall cleave unto his wife: and they shall be one flesh" (Genesis 2:24).

Never lose sight of the need you have for each other. Always remember that your spouse completes you in a way no one else can. No friend, no child, no parent—as wonderful as they may be—can do more for you than your spouse. So cleave to that one alone. Pursue the marriage relationship with a singular determination that will eventually make you one flesh—not just in concept but in fact.

There they are, the seven "C's" of a great relationship. Study them. Think about them. But most importantly...live by them. And discover the riches God has prepared for those who dare to become "heirs together in the grace of life!"

Prayer for Salvation and Baptism in the Holy Spirit

Heavenly Father, I come to You in the Name of Jesus. Your Word says, "...whosoever shall call on the name of the Lord shall be saved" (Acts 2:21). I am calling on You. I pray and ask Jesus to come into my heart and be Lord over my life according to Romans 10:9-10. "If thou shalt confess with thy mouth the Lord Jesus, and shalt believe in thine heart that God has raised him from the dead, thou shalt be saved." I do that now. I confess that Jesus is Lord, and I believe in my heart that God raised Him from the dead.

I am now reborn! I am a Christian—a child of Almighty God! I am saved! You also said in Your Word, "If ye then, being evil, know how to give good gifts unto your children: HOW MUCH MORE shall your heavenly Father give the Holy Spirit to them that ask him?" (Luke 11:13). I'm also asking You to fill me with the Holy Spirit. Holy Spirit, rise up within me as I praise God. I fully expect to speak with other tongues as You give me the utterance (Acts 2:4).

(Begin to praise God for filling you with the Holy Spirit. Speak those words and syllables you receive—not in English. You have to use your own voice. God will not force you to speak.)

Now you are a Spirit-filled believer. Continue with the blessing God has given you and pray in tongues each day. You'll never be the same!

About the author

Mac Hammond pastors Living Word Christian Center in Minneapolis, Minnesota. What began as a small gathering of believers in 1981 is now a 4,000-member congregation. He and his wife, Lynne, have been married 27 years and have three children.

For ministry information or a free tape catalog write to Living Word Christian Center, 7325 A Aspen Lane, Brooklyn Park, Minn. 55428, or call 612-424-2756.

For more information about this ministry and a free catalog, please write:

Kenneth Copeland Ministries
Fort Worth, Texas 76192

World Offices of
Kenneth Copeland Ministries

Kenneth Copeland
Post Office Box 1426
Parramatta
NEW SOUTH WALES 2124
AUSTRALIA

Kenneth Copeland
Post Office Box 830
RANDBURG
2125
REPUBLIC OF SOUTH AFRICA

Kenneth Copeland
Post Office Box 15
BATH
BA1 1GD
ENGLAND

Kenneth Copeland
Post Office Box 58248
Vancouver
BRITISH COLUMBIA
V6P 6K1
CANADA